D0916419

WALKING
AWAY
FROM
EXPLOSIONS
IN
SLOW
MOTION

WALKING AWAY FROM EXPLOSIONS IN SLOW MOTION

GREGORY CROSBY

To LAURA—
SEE YOU SOON BETWEEN
CREELY + CRUZ!

WARM REGARDS,

the operating system community print//document

WALKING AWAY FROM EXPLOSIONS IN SLOW MOTION

ISBN: 978-1-946031-33-4
Library of Congress Control Number: 2018948570
copyright © 2018 by Gregory Crosby
cover and typography design by Lynne DeSilva-Johnson
interior typesetting by Michael Flatt

For additional questions regarding reproduction, quotation, or to request a pdf for review contact operator@theoperatingsystem.org

This text was set in Europa, Gill Sans, Minion, DK Kaikura, and OCR-A Standard.

Books from The Operating System are distributed to the trade by SPD/Small Press Distribution, and/or with ePub and POD via Ingram, with production by Spencer Printing, in Honesdale, PA, in the USA.

The operating system is a member of the Radical Open Access Collective, a community of scholar-led, not-for-profit presses, journals and other open access projects. Now consisting of 40 members, we promote a progressive vision for open publishing in the humanities and social sciences. Learn more at: http://radicaloa.disruptivemedia.org.uk/about/

Your donation makes our publications, platform and programs possible! We <3 You.
bit.ly/growtheoperatingsystem

2018-19 OS SYSTEM OPERATORS
CREATIVE DIRECTOR/FOUNDER/MANAGING EDITOR: Lynne DeSilva-Johnson
DEPUTY EDITOR: Peter Milne Greiner
CONTRIBUTING EDITORS: Kenning JP Garcia, Adrian Silbernagel
JOURNEYHUMAN / SYSTEMS APPRENTICE: Anna Winham
SOCIAL SYSTEMS / HEALING TECH: Curtis Emery
VOLUNTEERS and/or ADVISORS: Adra Raine, Alexis Quinlan, Clarinda McLow, Bill Considine, Careen Shannon, Joanna C. Valente, Michael Flatt, L. Ann Wheeler, Jacq Greyja

the operating system
Brooklyn, NY
www.theoperatingsystem.org

For my mother
{who waited a very long time}

&

For Abigail
{without whom none of it would matter}

CONTENTS

II

III

ACKNOWLEDGMENTS

Desert Companion "Apologia for Pat Benatar"
"Voyeur"
"The Other Shoe is a Severed Foot"
"A Volta"
"Gregory Crosby Marked Himself Safe
During the Violent Incident
at Las Vegas, Nevada"

Flapperhouse "Nine Masks"

Fog Machine "Lachrymorpheus"

Gargoyle "Walking Away From Explosions
in Slow Motion"

Hyperallergic "The Hardest Working Lazy
Apartment Poem"

Linden Avenue "The Revelator"

Luna Luna "In Memory of When I Cared"
"You Say Chiasmus, I Say Chimera"
"They Were Singing *Rhiannon*, Not *Vienna*"

Posit "The Marquis of Sad"

"Solstice Goddamn"

Still "A Dog Barks in the Distance"

Yes Poetry "Empitaph"
"This Week in Hate"
"The Petition"

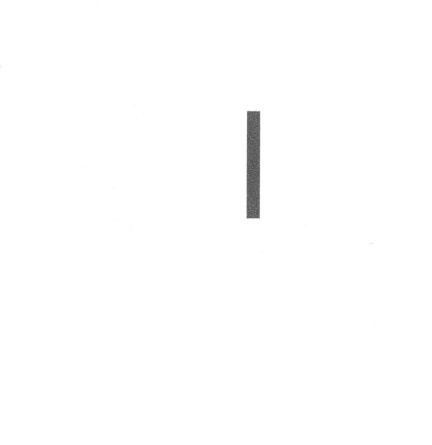

A DOG BARKS IN THE DISTANCE

The sounds that animals are made to make in picture books:
the sound of a bear talking in its sleep, of a rooster

that only crows in dreams, & the caw of a crow that roosts
in dreams, a crow that is neither black nor white, that's no

color at all except for the color of its voice.
The sound an old horse makes with just its eyes when you ask,

Why the long face? Or the dog you alternately kick
& rescue, in that place your mind goes to when you think

about how the world is full of other living things,
how the world is positively lousy with living things:

the sound that dog makes that frees & condemns in the same *woof.*
The dog that *barks in the distance,* the mangy trope that signifies

loneliness, all its illusion & promise (although,
sometimes, it's only there to let you know that nothing is

happening so something can). Everyone hears that dog;
no one's ever seen it. Everyone pictures a different

dog, purebred perhaps, more likely a mutt, the blessed
mutt that redeems with all its fuzziness, its dark eyes

looking up as its nose falls to earth like a shooting star.
That dog's bark, desolate & safe, beyond howl or growl...

A courtesy, like the sounds that humans are made to make,
talking in our sleep, clearing our throats to say *good morning*

to no one.

BUT THAT SHIP HAS SAILED

It was an accident, of course, the kind
that makes you say, *There are no accidents.*
You thought, *Let's see where the day takes us,*
but that's all days ever do, take & take,
until the sky's the color of a paint chip
that you'll never be able to match,
something you keep holding up to the light
only to think, *No, no, that's not quite it.*

But it is. You say you'll know it when you
see it, but that ship has sailed. All the ships
have sailed. They crisscross the horizon
while the wave sucks the sand from under
your feet. Almost a pleasant sensation,
the sunset. *Only an accident,* they'll say.

WALKING AWAY FROM EXPLOSIONS
IN SLOW MOTION

It's all you can do. The world is always
behind you, the catastrophe of time,
the exchange of air & fire, the wave
of force raising the hair on the back of
your neck, a rivulet of sweat unseen
by all the eyes on your unseeing gaze,
the blank face that says *I'm walking away,*
I'm getting away with something: all those

opportunities to find your body
framed by boiling galaxies of flame,
untouched by shrapnel, not above it all
but out in front of it, like the *future*
itself, walking *away*. Fucking *badass*.
Fuck no you don't look back; you can't look back.
A cinder in your eye might ruin the shot.
A world might suddenly taste of salt.

LONELY STARBUCKS LOVERS

To the sidewalk, all snowflakes look alike.
Accumulation, the hourglass sighs.
The blizzard is the life. We trudge flat white
to enjoy a Flat White. Breath precedes us,
the breath of white. The line for the bathroom,
indistinguishable from the line for
life. Someone is writing down the wrong name
on an empty cup. An empty mitten

picks up a tiny, trusting hand. A girl sings,
Lonely Starbucks lovers to an old man
who declaims, *Taylor Swift doesn't exist.*
She's a myth. It's all a myth, everywhere
you look. Milk foams, apocalyptic whoosh.
White on green, time drifts. Covers us. We kiss.

The thing about time is that it's *chronic*.
Better get out of sundown before town,
before the dead light devours those wolves,
the hours that hunt you higher, lower,
than high & low can know. The gardening
never ends: the pruning, the *where-it's-at*
that's clipped from nowhere, & then it's night,
again, stars unseen against the carnival
of light bleed. What are you really made of
if not this, this stupid brick? Out of sorts,
under the covers, the bed a black box
for recording dreams. Trains of thought, the cars
full of darkness. You could live a 1,000,000.
You won't. Time is stride: you, a stumble.

APOLOGIA FOR PAT BENATAR

You say love is a battlefield, & have
the choreography to prove it, but
it isn't. Blasted trees, gouged earth, people
who were once other than things, a silence
that's a type of blasphemy, where death
is depthless; a field of vision from which
all dimensions save one have been removed,
a flattening & then a fattening,

slaughter's self-fulfilling prophecy:
that's a battlefield. But have it your way.
One foot on the parapet, gun in hand.
Waiting for the signal to go over
the top. It's okay. Most soldiers don't know
what they're fighting for until it's too late.

LACHRYMORPHEUS

Amy asks, *Why isn't there a word for*
crying in a dream? Lachrymorpheus,
I glibly reply. Nick says, *Most people*
live a life of desire instead of
life itself. Everything's a fix, I nod.
Eternally, the Baron writes, *And I*
should see you again as I saw you…
You of whom I try in vain to say

nothing here… The second-person is
uncommon, I tell my students. Why might
you choose it? And a student raises her
hand: *To put you into the story. To*
make it happen to you. & my pillow
is wet. & I can't remember why.

BLUEBEARD HAS A SHAVE

In the chair, listening to the razor's
tango with the strop, he wonders what, precisely,
his problem is. The hot towel, blinding white,
slowly takes on the hue (thanks to his vanity & dye),
of a baby boy's blanket. Staring at the cracks
in the ceiling, he asks himself, *Why?*
They were lovely, mostly. Some were very shy.
Others more than held their own; the third one
even checkmated him once, her eyebrow arched
triumphantly, her smile wry. So why?
It seems there's a room inside his mind
he must never enter.

He watches the bare bulb flaring the top
of the barber's bald head, & suddenly
can't remember how it was the first one
came to die. There was no secret for her
to uncover. The chamber was empty back then.
Wasn't it? His brow furrows as the edge
scrapes his skin, the taut softness of his neck.
There must have been a reason, he reasons,
unaware of the key in his pocket, how it throbs

like an artery, a pulse dimly dreaming
of a slippage just beyond its consciousness:
a storm of steel, out there, beyond reason or reasons,
waiting to make heavy weather out of the calm
mirror of his heart. So, asks the barber
(steady stroke upon stroke), *What do you think
of the Ravens' chances this year?*

I don't follow, murmurs Bluebeard. I don't
follow, murmurs the key, a whorl of red rising
silently to the worn & worried surface
of its implacable, orderly teeth.

This is how it is to suddenly feel old:
hands removing the rings from your fingers
before your corpse is cold. It began
around the time that Tower Records closed,
& now it's reached escape velocity.
It's a quotidian atrocity,
worse than the grinding gears of penury,
this being rooted in the twentieth
century. I never smoked weed but only
because I never smoked at all, a vow
made when small that's all I carry
into the oblivious now, present
& absent as a quantum mechanic.
Dreams, they compartmentalize my life.
History is made to seem unfair, & so
it is. In an interview, a woman
says *dope* & *baller* in the same sentence,
& together they sound like an august
firm, a growing commercial concern,
in which one can do a form of penance,
an awesomely rad & fab & grotty
penance, the groovy bomb at the tip of
your tongue exploding into *What? What? What?*
I repent nothing. I confess less.
Clueless is as clueless does. Also silence.

MID-LIFE

Nel mezzo del cammin di nostra vita...

Forget I said anything, forget I
said everything. I'm a new translation,
like a version, read for the very first time.
I'm re-recorded, covered, recovered,
never before released, an alternate
track, first time available on this
obsolete format. A checklist, checked off.
Only the most assiduous collectors
care; only the professors, gathering
fuel for the long winters of their lives.
I'm the book with curvature of the spine,
an imposture, imposter & poster
child for all that I'll never need be.
I am father to the man, and to The Man.
My voice rings out only when my lungs
are filling with the black water called I.
(You can tell the water's black because, look,
all those stars! *That's* where they've been hiding!)
In my old school tie, my star-dust jacket,
I'm a franchise awaiting its reboot,
a remake, a based on, a suggested by.
The eraser is *crazy* about me.
So is the pencil. They can't wait. They just
can't *wait.*

THE SOUL, OR WHATEVER

The phrase *friendly ghost* is so, uh, *haunting*.
Is the house ever flattered by spirits
who refuse to depart? Does the ghost who
carries its head in its hands ever say,
*Hey, I was only holding this for someone
else.* The police kick in the door & there
you are, left holding the bag, that empty
body, existence. Or maybe it's not.
Maybe there are a few crumbs in the bottom,
& you just have to reach deeper, fumbling,
grasping. If only you could shake it out,
the body, but it mysteriously
refuses to upend itself. Only
time can do that. Only a creaking board,
a whisper as white as a sheet of paper,
will make you jump out of your skin at last.

MEMOIR

I changed all the names, not that it mattered.
Everyone sees right through those screens, *Me, You.*
Everyone wants what's only their due:
the heart that's bruised, the mind that's battered,
the body that's whole because it's shattered.
The truth is at its best when it's untrue,
which is to say, *disloyal.* It's a coup.
It overthrows the lies that gathered

in the mirror, in a glance both backward
& new. There's so much to keep to oneself.
There's a mirror that can only be said,
not so much cracked as hopelessly fractured.
There's nothing, no thing, to keep to oneself.
In the mirror's place there's a name instead.

The mirror speaks, & having spoken, does not move on.
You can only tell it, *You are ridiculous*
so many times before it's not you speaking at all.
A man's style is his mind's voice, says a beveled soul.
Everything you are slides away to the edges.
Everything you were falls away to the surface.
All of light bends to a whisper: *Say nothing of this.*
The mirror speaks. Better it should have kept silent.
Better it should have kept its own counsel, its own
wisdom, the kind that only comes from never learning
a single thing, repeated to infinity,
a single thing, repeated to infinity.

PROOF OF CONCEPT

Perhaps all the suffering, the joy,
the boredom punctuated by possibility,
the puncturing & inflating, the Future
of the Past & the Future's Past, has been
nothing more than a proof of concept.

If you wear the wrong color in front
of a Chroma key screen, you disappear.
This is why I always try to wear black,
which will only be a problem in the void.
Here, now, in the world, it's fine, although

you can't ever really see just what it is
(& it is what it is) that's projected
behind you. Maybe in post-production.
Maybe in the theater, unless you are
uncomfortable with seeing yourself.

The Chroma key screen of Wikipedia
declares that *proof of concept* means
*a realization of a certain
method or idea to demonstrate
its feasibility.* I resist

the urge to edit *a realization*
into the phrase *to manifest.* I wonder
why this urge is not a compulsion.
I wonder what is manifest, & what is
manifested. I wonder what's on the screen

behind me. Perhaps all the dreaming,
all the writing, the possibilities
foreclosed & forewarned, the desire
to be seen & unseen, has been nothing
less than what it is. Green screen, blue screen,

a leaf against the sky.

The only mystery is that there is
no mystery. Colonel Mustard, in the
Conservatory, with a Revolver;
Miss Scarlet, in the Comments, with a Meme.
What do these people do all day? Wonder,
or Don't Wonder, with an Hour to Kill.
Reflect, in the Moment, with a Sigh.
A clue is an invitation to the

void. Every envelope is born empty.
Every experience is an out of
Boddy experience. What do you do
when no corpse turns up? When the day unfolds
according to appearances? When you
know, with each breath you take, whodunit?

SEVEN IMPOSSIBLE THINGS BEFORE BREAKFAST

"A turtle carries its grave on its back."
A tornado is a grave that just can't
stay put. Paper is electricity
that blows around, untouched by the wind.
Now, the problem with a voice out of the
whirlwind is that no one can make out
the words above the roar. Then there's the
alarming eclipse of the self (alarming
because it never lasts). You drink Victory
at Sea until you drown the war itself.
Off in the distance, above the voices,
The Yardbirds' "For Your Love" is playing,
& the shadow of the turtle falls slowly,
slowly, across your short stack of pancakes.

WE'LL BE BACK IN JUST A MOMENT, BUT FAUST . . .

What am I supposed to do with a mad scientist for an hour,
asks the Prisoner of the Lost Universe, & what can I
say? At this time of day, it's always Civilization
vs. The Atom. I say, Your brain is too feeble
to understand what I have accomplished in the realm
of Science. You're a dreamer, Doc, says the world, & money
is bad for dreamers. But it's mine, I whisper, mine by right
of discovery. No one may see it & live. No one does.
Frankenstein might meet the Space Monster, but he doesn't
invite him in. Jesse James might meet Frankenstein's Daughter,
but it's only a coffee date. Mad? Is one who has solved
the secret of life to be considered mad? Well... I tampered
in God's domain, & you can't play God. *But somebody has to!*
That always gets a big laugh. Maniacal, you might say.
My darling, I failed. I meddled in things man must leave alone.
Also in things God must leave alone. You dare to call me
mad? I should be so lucky, says the Brain That Would Not Die.

LAST CALL AUBADE

The evening climbs down from the sky.
Dawn stares at the summit, mouth dry.
Easy as walking,
stupid as talking,
the mocking, & the lie.

When I was young, I knew something
about what I was becoming,
but now I have found
that where I was bound
is just a sound, a crushing.

The ascent brings nothing closer.
The song, it knows no composer.
Easy as breathing,
silent as wreathing,
a seething, & a closure.

Everyone imagines the Rapture as
instantaneous, but what if angels
have a very different sense of time?
Seeing as how they stand outside of it.
What if that sweet chariot is swinging
not low but slow, & the rising of the tides,
the disappearance of the ice, is all
we'll know or need to know, as the moment,
coming forth to carry us into the
only home we've ever unknown, beyond
without back, expands like the universe
itself into billions & billions of
stars over billions & billions of years,
with everyone saved, everyone left behind?

SOMETHING TO FALL BACK ON

A cloud's shadow is a type
of cloud, but one rarely says
this out loud, & never in front

of fog, which always takes offense
somehow, likely because fog
would like to think itself

a cloud, would like to be castles
& dragons & cities & your mom,
but it isn't, it's just fog,

everywhere & nowhere, a curtain
that only lifts when the play
is over. You can't mollify

it. You can't say, *Shadows only
wish they were you.* It won't
believe you. Meanwhile, a cloud

glances down, seeing nothing
but a cloud atop another
cloud. Clouds, it thinks. It's clouds,

all the way down. It's clouds,
thinks fog. Nothing but clouds,
all the way up. The shadows

wisely think about nothing,
like the sun, although the
nothing the sun thinks about

is the supermassive black
hole at the center of the
Milky Way. It's a good thought,

thinks the sun, shining away.
It's something to fall back on,
a shadow, all the way down.

ARE YOUR HEADACHES JUST A DEAD TWIN INSIDE YOUR BRAIN?

All those times, saying *It's not a tumor*
in an Austrian accent,
while something drove a nail
into the wall behind your eyes, shut tight.

All those times in a darkened room,
listening to the throb
& sob of that little voice.
Hair, bone, teeth. Curls, a weak chin, braces.

The day came when you actually needed
a hole in your head,
& they found her,
tiny teratoma, which sounds like a girl

you knew in high school, *Hi, I'm Tera,*
Tera Toma! Are you
signing up for Key Club?
I just know we're going to be besties!

But nobody is best friends forever, not even
those you consumed
in the womb.
That little voice, always whispering,

Wonder Twin powers, activate... form of
a question unasked,
shape of an absence.
Hair, bone, teeth. *At least there wasn't*

an eye, you shudder & sigh, while somewhere deep
in the cells,
there's a lid, twitching,

in endless sleep, helplessly dreaming
the dream, tapping it out like a sailor
trapped in a submarine.
Hair, bone, teeth.
Hair, bone, teeth. Hair, bone, teeth.

CHINA CAN'T STOP PEOPLE FROM HIRING FUNERAL STRIPPERS

They say you can always fall back on your shadow,
even in the dark, & it's true, but what about
the tragedy of the fish that's obsessed with water?
Every arrow in the quiver is Time's Arrow,
& every bow is Clara. Films are no longer
film, & it takes a half-hour for a Polaroid
to develop because it's not a Polaroid.
When we descend from the train to get on the bus,
we are surrounded by tombstones etched by lasers,
portraits of all the targets the arrow's passed by,
every one a bulls-eye. Perhaps you'll have sex
on my grave, like Mary & Percy. Perhaps you'll
do a little dance. Perhaps, at long last,
I'll be able to keep my hands to myself.

LEARNING TO BE DISAPPOINTED IN A NEW WAY

First, you give up all your cynicism
in favor of a dull sincerity,
a butter knife held to the throat of life.
Then you speak of yourself as a person
of bad faith, & demand toleration.
Next, you examine all you know nothing
about, & give your all to the discourse.
You do not speak of rights, privileges.
You speak of rivers & borders & guards.
You circle the wagons & then complain
that you're so *bored* with this endless waiting.
You still wait. At last, you ask the bodies,
What did you expect? Then you turn away,
calling, *Hey! Somebody come close their eyes!*

THE GLASS DELUSION

The people who think they are made of glass
usually focus on their fragility
rather than a sense of transparency,
but I was preoccupied by the sand:
the sense that I had been fused & not born.
Neither a solid nor a liquid, but
both. A window in a safety coffin,
dead perhaps alive, alive perhaps dead.
A feeling that I was very useful,
very dispensable, both warm & cool
to the touch. Human, I guess. There are those
who describe this state as a delusion.
I sit in my frame between warm breath, rain.
I imagine the branch, tapping, the palms
pressed against my body, the eyes, seeing,
unseeing, & think, *A hairline fracture.*
A spider's web of the provisional.
A surface as smooth & false as Providence.
A shard held gingerly, catching the light.

WE'LL BE THE DEATH OF ME

Consider this poem the drunk dial
from the ex you never had. Often, when
I'm home alone, only the thought of how
my dead body might be found keeps me from
loving you. I'm reading a book in bed
entitled *Today in Wishful Thinking*.
I read a red page & I paint it blank.
No, we will never think of each other
at the same time. We will never think of
anything not to say. We will never
shut up about the silence we obey.
It's okay. You can safely ignore this
text. Claim that you didn't see it
until later. It's later. It's too late.

NOT SAFE FOR WORK

Not safe for unemployment. Not safe for
sleeping until noon. Not safe for the dreams
you remember when you sleep until noon.
Does it really matter, whether your life
is ruined by something that didn't happen
or by something that did? Not safe for time,
not safe for space, not safe for dimensions
beyond this, not safe for parallel universes
or universes that might someday meet.
Not safe, not safe. Stranger danger is
stranger, but friend danger is strangest yet.
If I held my enemies any closer,
they'd be behind me. They might be, yet.
Do not open this. Someone's standing there.

He said, *Everyone was so nice to me,*
I almost didn't go through with it.

How terrible the edge, the margin of
air between bodies, between the open

windows, perpetual summer days, &
the windows painted over, painted shut.

From hopeless rooms, night appeared only as
a cross across his blood, where all the stars

are aligned & out of joint. The demon
leaves the body so slowly, glacially,

like that little bird that rubbed its beak
against the mountain's peak, & by the time

the mountain was gone, that was one second
in hell. Hell is always with us, & still

they forgive. They express their forgiveness,
though he didn't ask for it. He can't ask

for it. The whole horror of history
stands behind him, & it can't ask for it.

They give it anyway. The bird snatches
a bit of song from the air & returns

its shiny little beak to the task.
One second. One second. One second.

NIGHT'S PLUTONIAN SHORE

New close-up images of Pluto from NASA's New Horizons spacecraft reveal a bewildering variety of surface features...

Who knew you had a heart so big, so cold.
Who knew you could forgive us anything—

demotion, distance—anything, except
a paparazzo nine years on your trail.

Out in the true dark, there's so little soul;
it's really not worth all this effort

to steal it. To come all this way, & then
just keep going. It's touching, really.

A little creepy, but mostly touching.
To come so far to come so close, all for

a glimpse, like a peeping tom who slips
from his perch & falls into the alley's abyss.

To say goodbye because you "need your space."
To look forward to a backward glance.

To invade the only privacy left.
To never having to say *nevermore*.

Spoiler alert: Your favorite characters
die. Huge jumps in time, years & years. One moment,
everyone's young; the next, middle aged, temples
sprayed with industrial gray. Turns out that,
in the end, no one is what they seem.
You don't see any of the twists coming.
The finale's final scene is a mystery
beyond puzzling: Where the hell are they?
What's that sound in the distance? Where's that
strange light coming from? What does the hero
mean when he whispers, *I think this is where
we came in*, & then vanishes? Why,
when the screen fades to black, are the credits
so hard to read? Little letters swim before
glazed eyes, binge-sweet & red-rimmed, while a strangled
voice, thrill-choked & trembling, asks *What shall we
watch next?* But whose voice is it? Nothing stirs
upon the couch. Nothing stirs outside, except
leaves budding, leaves falling. Whole seasons,
dumped. Something whispers, *Six seasons & a movie*.
The wind picks up, rises, dies. *Six seasons
& a movie*. Your blue hand, clutching mine.

THE PHANTOM TIME HYPOTHESIS

I was my own imaginary friend, forever telling
myself not to sit there, lest I be crushed (I was always
crushed). I spoke in a creaturely voice, a little monster
stitched together out of materials not found in nature.
Under the table, I watched as the war broke out between
idols graven from plastic, so many voices, all at once.
I claimed I was afraid of the dark so I could read comics
by the duck-shaped dark nite of my soul lite. I was something
that never happened, yet kept happening: a conspiracy
called "child." I grew up. I became that invisible friend,
all the voices blended into one, forever telling
my troubles, forever asking is it okay if I can
come with: to ice cream, to the toy store, to wherever
this is, this neverland that can't exist & still does.

The inflation of an air mattress as
self-fulfilling prophecy. Singing
R.E.M.'s "Catapult" but replacing
catapult in the refrain with *laundromat*.
A Ziploc bag big enough to crawl into.
It's just life. That vague feeling of being
punished is simply being itself. *Don't
tell me how to feel*; I know, but sometimes
it's myself I'm telling. Tiny disasters
strung like Xmas lights on the Tree of Life,
a wreath of everblacks on the front door.
Welcome. Go Away. The thing about a
threshold is the pain: the Venn diagram
where you recognize what *home* overlaps.

THE CONDOLENCES

Sometimes we speak to make the bears dance;
sometimes we sing a lullaby to lull them
into their long, long sleep, the longest sleep,
the winter where all your loved ones are kept
close, even though you can only see them
in your dreams. So sorry, so, so very
sorry for your loss, so sorry to hear
this, our thoughts & prayers, prayers & thoughts,

so sorry, hang in there, sorry, very
sad & sorry news, if you need any
one, thing, ear, so sorry to hear, sorry,
very sad & sorry to see, to hear,
in our hearts, keeping you there, so very
sorry, your loss, so sorry, so very
sorry, so so so so so so sorry,
sorry, shhh, sleep now,

big bear, little bear.

PHOENIX, 3 JULY

You know, you really haven't lived until
you've stood in a room with your dead brother.

My mother didn't break down, but I did,
& I didn't pull myself together

until I heard her voice, broken but not,
tell him, "You were a good son. We love you."

This isn't what I meant to say. I meant
to tell you that it's not too late to run

away & join the circus, like I did,
long ago. That's where I am when I seem

far away.

The relief, the strange mercy, that my
brother still looked like himself even when

he was no longer himself. His lips,
slightly parted. His teeth. The quality

of his dreamless eyelids. His white beard, still
flecked red because nothing had been done to him--

the flames

were waiting, but my mother could not, she
could not, she could not, she could not, until

she had seen him. I meant to tell you what
I said, after my mother left me there

alone with him, to "say goodbye." I wish
I could say, could tell you what I said,

could tell you how I said goodbye, but
I'm grabbing a trapeze bar in mid-air.

That's my head, there, inside the lion's jaws;
my face, pressed against the clown car's window.

That's my tinsel, my sawdust, choking my
throat, stinging my eyes. That's my flaming hoop,

my lastly-through-a-hogshead-of-real-fire.
Here I am, falling not falling, jumping

through it.

WING, PRAYER

The pilot said, "We're beginning our descent,"
& I thought, yes, that's right, wheels down, waiting
for the jolt that brings the monster back to
life. Outside it's white; down, down through the clouds,
the all of it, hidden. I'm beginning
my descent, unable to remember
how I came to be in flight. I'm going
to ground. I'm coming down. Soon, we'll all be

touching down. You know, don't you, what they made
the monster from. How am I to spend this,
having browsed Sky Mall, read my thriller, drank.
Attendants, prepare for landing; angels,
sing me to my best. The roar is all I
hear, surrounded by strangers, by tears.

A joke came out of a cloud of clove smoke:
Heaven or Las Vegas? We always said
Vegas, of course, although we knew better.
Here, no one need try to get to the bar;
there was always another bar beyond
the next bank of slots, always another
ninety-nine cent breakfast beyond the clocks.
It was nineteen hundred & ninety-three,
& we were free to ponder how synthpop
didn't require a synthesizer.
It was a state of mind, a rocket set
to drift & fire, fire & drift.
"Otherworldly" might not mean what you think.
It might be the dream you were born to leave.

It might be the dream you were born to leave,
but that didn't imply you were awake.
Today, when I see a sheet of tin foil,
I think of the windows, & those who slept
all day, rising into the graveyard shift.
This just in: Bela Lugosi's still dead.
I listened to that single on cassette,
driving with a dead girl to a party,
though she wasn't truly dead, not yet.
I was wearing my strangest costume yet:
the prodigal. I had spent all summer
in the British Bulldog's poker-lit dark
with a pint of Peter Gabriel's "Blood
of Eden." I remembered everything.

Of Eden, I remembered everything:
the rattle of the cable car, the hills,
City Lights, & Lilith's embittered voice,
reminding me that this was not, in fact,
a garden, unless it was Gethsemane.
But that's perhaps too melodramatic.
Suffice to say I was dust, not golden;
I'd gotten myself back to the desert,
like all the good billion year old carbon
copies of failure. It is indeed hard
to tell when all your love's in vain (or insane).
All my vinyl, my books, my clothes, even
my name (once short, now long): behind me
now. In front of me, the pitiless sun.

Now, in front of me, the pitiless sun,
the Nth degrees of the rest of my days,
one hundred & ten in the absent shade
(how could they have built this city without
arcades?), wondering if I was reborn
or just cleverly undead. Twenty-five
years old, The Sands not yet shifted, The Dunes
soon doomed, implosion upon implosion.
There was still time, & there was Still Time,
the iris wide & full of light. I was
home, question mark. I was home, full stop.
From the land beyond Beyond, from the sea
past hope & fear, I bid the djinni,
Appear, & tell me: how should I appear?

Appear! Tell me, yes, how should I appear,
here where every window is a mirror?
So I looked into eyes instead & saw
what there was, & wasn't, to be seen.
To be seen suddenly became all of me.
I inserted myself into the scene,
or, if you prefer, The Scene. I made some
noise. I played the fool, the fop, the poet,
the "professor" who had never received
a degree, twenty-five going on fifteen.
I chased "girls." I caught a glimpse or two
(or three). I tried (as Al the Inland Sailor
advised) to "redeem the time," not knowing
that time cannot be redeemed, only spent.

That time cannot be redeemed, only spent:
well, that's Vegas. *I lost three hundred bucks.*
Yeah, but did you have a good time? Vegas,
the only place where you can have a good time
without actually enjoying yourself.
My favorite joke. *If life is a joke,*
shouldn't it at least be a funny one?
When I was young, I knew the answer to this.
I'll never come home the way I did then,
never again know so little or so
much. The graveyard shift never ends but it
does shift, from necropolis to neon
& back again, where everyone lies still,
waiting to hear a coin that never drops.

Waiting to hear a coin that never drops:
instead, the slots print out a scrip to be
redeemed at the cage marked CHANGE. Turn, & face
the mundane. I left, I saw, I came, I
left. I changed. Home is the place where, when you
die, they let you live long enough to say
goodbye. To forgive something, if not yourself.
The place where nothing ever happens so
anything can. The place that's *the next best thing
to leaving* (Remember? No? That's okay).
It's always nineteen-ninety-three somewhere.
A homecoming never begins or ends.
Your city lies in dust, my friend... but you
don't (a joke out of cloud of clove smoke).

I KEEP IT TOGETHER BY FALLING APART

I keep it together by falling apart.
The streets are my sanatorium rest,
the day to day my failed stress test.
All my breakdowns break down before they start;
the heart attack wants what the heart hearts,
but cannot have it, not yet. I am blessed
with the curse of the waylaid wedding guest,
forced to listen to the Story of Art:

mimesis, catharsis, boredom & void.
I will never arrive to stop the bride
from making her final, futile mistake.
I am her fortress & I am destroyed,
the little voice that squeaks, *At least I tried.*
I win, every time. *Please, give me a break.*

THE PHOTO THAT MY GIRLFRIEND TOOK OF ONE OF HER RIDING STUDENTS HUGGING A HORSE & THEN EMAILED TO ME,

it wrecks me. It ruins me. Something in
me shatters & escapes into the air,
a broken ampoule filled with the opposite
of poison. Her eyes closed, her hand on his nose,
the nostril bigger than her thumb, her face
balked & comforted by her huge white
helmet, the helmet tipped back a little,
pressed against the horse's face, blue halter
framing the slope of brown & white, the steel
ring gleaming in the light, & her lips
against the muzzle in not quite a kiss,
chin out, almost in defiance, nuzzling
the hot breath of the evidence, the proof
of life as other, truly other. Eyes,
closed; the horse's eyes high & away,
outside the frame. Her serene little face.
The wordless, worthless prayer given worth
because wordless, because it is & isn't
prayer. Something in me hopes she never
opens her eyes, her hand never falls away
from the snort & sigh of the world as it
breathes, just breathes, both ready & at rest.
Is this kitsch? I don't care. *Kitsch is what one*
responds to, helplessly. How the world catches
us, unaware; how we are released.

HOME OF THE BOTTOMLESS CUP

No one commits a murder before their
first cup of coffee. Very light & sweet,
the body, after you've stirred its darkness,
waiting for it to cool so that you don't
burn the vault of heaven on the first sip.
The second cup never even comes close.
Black as hell, strong as death, sweet as love.
Black as time, strong as time, sweet as time,

morning's the abyss of pure potential
& dread. It warms your hands while you freeze
into the present's permanent moment.
It's the dream you drink until it turns cold,
the horizon you can't reach because you're
already there, the corpse you kill, & revive.

FOUND POEM LOST

All women have been corrupted by the bikini,
sayeth the Internet, but the Bikini was corrupted first
by a hydrogen bomb named Castle Bravo (applause).

I often think of the expression on John Calvin's face
when he died, & fell toward the light, & then
discovered for himself what predestination truly is.

A human being is an animal that always thinks
it's both much better & much worse than it really is.
You might describe this as humanity's "Original Sin."

There are no correct interpretations: only those that are
plausible & persuasive, or implausible, unpersuasive.
Or, alas, implausible & entirely persuasive.

Of course, if God is everywhere, then God is nowhere as well.
If everything's a swimming costume, nothing goes naked.
Sweet corruption, give me Bikini Body before I die.

8.

Of course, the first thing she did was change her
number. The tune took longer, years in fact.
She'd had it drummed into her by the moon,
by all the wayward lessons of jazz, tap.
There's still a picture of her in the hall
in costume for Madame's School of the Dance.
Stars, glitter, pink spandex, a cigarette
hidden in her left glove, beaming with love
for no one, nothing in particular,
except for the shiny surfaces of
self. When winter came she slept in her skates.
She imagined a nation watching her
skirt as it flared & spun, & a nation
did, a silent, violent stare, its mouth dry.

6.

A silent, violet stare, her mouth so dry
after an evening of drinking, her face
purple in the blacklight, neon crescent
of her chin in the velvety darkness
that smelled of smoke, sweat & soft coercion,
the pleading that resembled a cop's
crocodile smile as he says *Please step out
of the car.* The only thing that keeps
everything from spinning are his hands,
but suddenly she wants to spin away,
out of the orbit of what's happening,
her mouth forming a word that becomes
a black hole, & the light cannot escape,
& the earth that will not swallow her up—

7.

The earth refuses to swallow her up.
Under the shower, she considers drowning,
how one darkness is good as another,
how her body is nothing but darkness
inside, how she wants her insides to claim
the too bright surface that blinds & binds her,
& then she has to go to work, so does.
Coffee, the train, the street, & everywhere
a conspiracy of clocks to tell her
everything changes, nothing goes away.
A whole shift spent sifting all the tortures
that he could suffer, should suffer, her eyes
welling with visions that she stuffs into
paper, plastic, her arm robotic with rage.

5.

Paper or plastic? Her arm robotic,
punching keys. Not what she'd had in mind,
back in the days of batons, SATs.
Before her mother's cancer, her father's
empire of empty bottles. She can still
see all the threads unraveling, the slow
implosion of dreams taken for granted,
& always in the lowest hours knowing
where the boys were, the ones who made it all
better by making it worse. It's a curse,
she told the mirror, but said it with a smirk.
As if she were immune from the feeling
she knew from others, the mundane terror
& exhaustion of walking through their gaze.

3.

The strange exhilaration of their gaze:
remembering the way that first head turned,
how his shag cut shifted as he tilted
his chin to acknowledge her, lips half-curled,
a shy leer. The next day he asked her out,
& she went, just thirteen to his eighteen—
the thrill of what almost but didn't happen
when he found out she *wasn't* sixteen,
the promise she made good on later
with someone else, & why not? Why not?
Remembering, the rage now curdling into
blame that spoke out from every surface,
every reflection. *No*, she would tell the girl
she was, wasn't. *Do not do this to yourself.*

0.

She was, wasn't. *Do not do this to yourself.*
But what was *this*? When the first call came,
the voice sick with something, *I need to make
you mine*, she felt her body turning away,
as if to say, *I don't know you; you
are on your own.* By the third call, she knew
that somewhere there was a wall, her body
written on it, her body *was* that wall,
that number, no matter how many times
she changed it. Late at night, long after
all the calls had ended, she dialed it,
& when her body answered, she hung up.
This went on through boyfriends, a husband.
Do not do this to yourself. What? Do what?

9.

Do not do this to yourself. So she stopped
one day, suddenly, like a wine glass dropped,
then swept up, forgotten. Her body asked
It wasn't me, was it? & she replied,
Oh, no, no, it wasn't you at all, no.
Something inside of her did figure-eights,
carefully now, over ice grown thin, thin,
but not yet cracked, & no, not "something," but
her body, which was hers again, limbs
stretching out, eyes wide, a tongue in her head
that began to move, to bear witness to
where the body, all these years, had been,
& just who, what, had been responsible.
She knew their walls. She had their numbers.

Nothing could be easier: the privilege
of silence, the fantasy of a world
in winter, wrapped in blankets of blankness,
paper that dissolves between your fingers,
leaving them wet with the opposite of
tears. One must have a mind of White-Out,
& have been wrong for long, long, long time.
Let others build a snowman; it's too cold.

Every time I speak I can see my breath,
& so I shut up, like a house intent
upon its hearth. I concentrate on spring,
which is always only arriving, never
quite here yet. I bring in more firewood.
I sit, shivering still, by the window.

EVEN THE BOSS MONSTERS OF THE DARK
ENLIGHTENMENT ARE WEAK BITCHES

Truth be told, she said, this *is* my first rodeo,
& then she broke apart into pieces of honeycomb,
which caught the last light as they fell across your path,
& you could taste each five-fold sweetness, even though
you'd cut out your own tongue in anticipation
of this moment. You carry it. You carry it
on your back, the way a hermit crab crawls into
a shell called The World & drags it across a beach
where every grain of sand is counted & forgotten.
Every sliver you ever dug out of a finger
was a piece of the True Cross; every stone passed
was an Infinity Gem, another wish flushed away.
All you ever paid attention to was the pain.
How many died & will die & cannot die to put
that sweetness in your mouth, sticking to the roof
of your palate above the empty room of your voice?
How many blind fish have you caught in your dark net?
How will you ever know if it was worth it, these crimes
you've committed in the name of freedom? Freedom
is a hive where every drone knows his name & nothing
else. In the dark, the sweetness waits. It's rotten;
it's perfect; it's still the word you will never say.

ALL THE PIERCED TONGUES IN PORN

The kind of success that isn't failure
but isn't really success. The sort of
pleasure that is only money, hovering
like a tiny drone outside the frame.
The manner of speaking that ends on a
question when all of the answers are plain.
The way a room is really brought together
by the memory of pain. The look in
the eyes, & the eyes unseen, that marks
a presence absent, an absence present.
The pressure of a thought on the soft
underside of a bland, recurring dream.
The category mistake that is language,
the taxonomy of release. The tiny hole
that is filled with a pebble polished
by a silent, silver torrent of speech.

A CALL TO SOMETHING

Tomorrow all the past. Paris is worth
an infinite Mass, but so is Beirut,
so is Raqqa, Damascus, & Baghdad,
visible cities, invisible dead.
The safest space is the emptiness of death,
except death is full, filling & brimming
with souls, or with the absence of soul.
It seems death has no beginning or end,

so where does this leave life? How do you kill
those who hope to kill you without becoming
death? How do you live in the dark of them?
They are not nameless, though they have no names.
They believe they will be seen by standing
in your light. You have no choice. You have no choice.

THE END OF DECEMBERS

Autumn accelerates. It is what it
isn't, it is what it shouldn't, it is
what it cannot, must not. A light inside
the unquiet, the disquiet, the *not quite*.
The Third World War; the Fourth Estate; the fifth,
emptied into a body desperate for sleep.
It's a world of trouble & here I sit,
making movies: dreaming in colors
while winter gray seeps from my eyes.
Demagogues warm their hands at the fires.
Our asteroid awaits in the distance,
in the dark. What would you do if you
only had X to live? The same as if
I only had Y. As if I had *why*.

OWITH!

Here's the catch: we aren't all in the same boat,
though it seems that way.

We are level with each other, but there's
open water between

us where once there was a deck. We're drifting.
Here's the catch in the

throat: the things I'd like to say but cannot.
I would have to shout

over a void of wave & fog that would
reveal wave & fog.

How would we bear the recognition—how
the provocative

can dwindle into merely vocative?
To say *O!* & watch

it slowly close instead of open?
To address the fog

where once your dark eyes flashed at the railing,
exclaiming, *Look! There's*

Orion. There's Venus, rising. Your hand
against the velvet;

my voice, an apostrophe caught, crushed,
forced together,

forced apart: *Owith! Owith! Owith!*
O, without—

"Someone stands on the beach in Santa Monica.
She dips an empty glass vial into the sea.
She carries it away to a waiting car; then
she drives across the country, & that's your life,
everything you are, the water in that vial,
& when she arrives in Coney Island, she walks
to the edge of the surf, & she opens the vial,
& pours you out into the Atlantic, & that's
death, & there you are, water into water,
salt into salt, ocean to ocean, & who could
ever find you again in all those waves? You think
there's still a someone in all that water who could
say, *I've never seen the ocean?*" Just then, "Ocean"
by the Velvet Underground came up on Shuffle.
There was a tremendous pause before our laughter
rolled over her, over the fire pit's distortion,
down the sand & into the dark sound of the sea,
whose voice we could never not hear & never see.

VOYEUR

What a perfect excuse, loneliness.
Sex & violence, the essence of this,
the confession that I do not confess.

I turn the lights on before I undress.
The mirror is something I cannot miss.
What a perfect excuse, this loneliness,

the most cherished thing that I possess.
It's a curdled rapture, a spoiled bliss,
a confession that I will not confess.

It's never the cause of my distress.
It seals my eyes with a lingering kiss.
What a perfect excuse is loneliness,

that risible, invisible caress.
So terrible, so apt. It's what I'll miss
when I confess what I cannot confess:

that you alone will make my heart fluoresce.
My love is the death you cannot dismiss.
What a perfect excuse, loneliness!
This is not a confession; I confess.

IN CAMERA, I WALK WITH YOU

V. once said, in a dream,
That camera only captures

the sound of her black silk
stockings, but she didn't

say it in one of my dreams,
but in one of hers, & I'm,

not sure if she said it,
of if I said it, or someone

else, some person or persona,
the known unknowns of bottomless

dream, said it; but now I
am holding that photograph

between my finger & thumb,
like the material, the seam,

of something I cannot touch,
cannot see, cannot descend

from thigh to knee, from was
to be, from nothing to is.

There is no record, no archive,
that cannot be faked—no

evidence, & no one
who needs to be convinced,

& yet, you have to take my
word on this. You have to

take me at my word.

LATE SHOW AT THE ORPHEUM

He looked back, &
she was there,

smiling shyly,
slyly, as if

they'd just met.
She did not

disappear. *Fuck
them*, she said.

*I'm not going
anywhere.*

He held out his
hand, & she took

it. Her hair took
on the sun as they

stepped out of
the last shadow

& into Day for
Night. Her hair,

a corona, afire.
Oh… oh. What light.

Everything
was fire.

It was the
lyre that

vanished.

BLUE, BLUE, ELECTRIC BLUE

David Bowie (1947-2016)

To be an alien is a common curse; to become one,
a singular gift. Always crashing in the same car,
always surviving that chrome chrysalis, the starlight
reflected one way in your left eye, another in your right.
You made something of yourself, as they say, & then you
made something else, performed your own sea-changes,
becoming
rich & strange & sometimes (always) human again, in the way
only humans can. A true aristocrat says, *You, too, can fall
to Earth.* All you have to do is listen to the dust falling
from the stars—ashes to ashes, lashes to lashes, surrounded
by starry shadows, glittering, still. I should be outside,
where the music is, where it goes on forever, listening
to the skies, trying for a glimpse of your possibilities…

But I don't want to go out. I want to stay in. Get things done.

THE MARQUIS OF SAD

I.

Freedom is melancholy; melancholy, freedom.
At least, that's what the weird sisters told me.

Once spoken, every word is true, even
all the words yoked to great chains of lies.

I never go down to the river for fear
of finding myself on the opposite bank,

not knowing how I came to be there,
miles from any crossing. But I can hear it.

I can hear the rocks suffering the rapids,
the teeming foam of my mind searching for

the tarn of Auber. It's always in the first
place you look, always in the very last line.

If I say my heart is heavy, it's because
my heart dowses water; the hidden spring

tugs at it like an impatient child. *Now?*
it asks. *Now? Then when? When? Are we there yet?*

II.

The Knight always stands in stark contrast
to Melancolia: his action & resolve opposed

to her pensive, passive hours, but look again
to his face beneath his helm. Look at his eyes.

He already feels the dragon's neck beneath
his boot heel & he's sorry to have ever heard

of damsels, princesses, sacrifices.
Look again at her face: the look of one who

goes to war knowing there is no victory,
only survival. Those who live to fight

another day know the days are endless...
days upon days, forever armed to the teeth.

III.

I know that the person who uses the word
escapist as a pejorative is most likely

a jailer. A cow caught running in the street
ahead of its slaughter date was returned

to the butcher who declined to kill it,
turning it over to a sanctuary

where no one is eaten by anything but
time. Once in a while, the universe is so

magnanimous that it breaks your heart in two.
It comes back to you, this story, whenever

you fire up the grill to the sound of your
empty stomach, the coals aching with red.

IV.

Here in the Bastille of Monday morning,
Sunday morning comes down with a fever,

dying for lack of water, a word of kindness.
From the cell of the warden's office, I rejoice.

When the rabble tear this week down, brick by brick,
this is what I will miss the most: the quiet

hour where I sign, with a flourish, another
letter of resignation that no one will accept.

V.

Everybody dies alone & that is beautiful.
Of course, it sounds funny when *you* sing it.

There are some gestures that can only be seen,
never felt. Unless you make them yourself.

Noblesse oblige requires me to tell you this.
Now, please, let me eat my cake; *here's a slice for you.*

Up here in my tower, the floor is made
of mist. I'm forever standing, falling,
trying to figure out which is which;
to figure out which word leaves my mouth
like the jagged bliss of a turned key.
How to say something to see something.
How to give voice to despair without
giving in to despair. How to give care
without caring, without carrying on.
Love might be the only reality,
but pain is more electable. Up here,
the air is both thin & thick, light-headed
& leaden. I can't find the stairs. I have
only this one vote, this secret ballot;
I abstain, I abstain, I abstain.

SUPER TUESDAY

Can you hear me now? The voice, not in our ears,
but near, nearer than we can imagine.
We ask questions to assess the damage.

We avoid gluten but gorge upon fear.
This is the feast that increases famine.
Can you hear me now? The voice, not in our ears,

but in our throats, our ravening careers
forever ascending, forever crashing.
We ask questions to assess the damage;

we survey the scene, eyes dimming with tears.
How could it, we cry. How could it happen.
Can you hear me now? The voice, not in our ears

but scrawled, supine, across screens, across years
of serene surmise, counterfeit compassion.
We ask questions to assess the damage;

we nod at the answers, so calm & austere.
We see them coming, teeth like blades, flashing.
Can you hear me now? The voice in our ear,
polling for answers, electing the damage.

All the witnesses in the world to come
will not keep it from happening again.
All the testimony will not prevent
future testimonies. Justice is so
fragile & so strong it might as well be
myth. No one can agree on who it was
that said, *Belief is an idea grown bald,*
but still we strew the streets with bodies
in order to possess a comb. Help me:
all that I have is piled sky-high, across
the mouths of these avenues, the barricades
that everyone simply walks right through.
When the revolution comes, it leaves, too.
When the words appear they are erasures.

INTENSE SEQUENCES OF PERIL

They're everywhere, causes seeking effects,
effects bewildered by causes, long chains
with missing links you can color in, dots
you can't connect because of the pattern
of the blood spatter: Forward, Impact, Void.
How we dance with History: light-footed,
yet stepping on our own toes, waiting for
someone, anyone, to cut in without

cutting into us. We watch with horror.
Horror never talks during the movie.
Horror waits for the lights to come up;
it wants to go for a drink & discuss.
Perilous times, yes. Plots, thickening.
History can always hear you breathing,
one sharp intake of breath after another.

FLASHLIGHT

What light suffers isn't much; it's
too quick to know itself, even

over the void, even if *the void*
is the wrong way to describe a

darkness. We're the ones who suffer
what light tells, from the candle

in a Caravaggio to that terrible
midnight text, diamonds cutting

new paths down our faces. Light
never suspects its heaviness, &

how we revel in its absence;
how, beneath blankets, we

celebrate our temporary mastery,
clicking it in & out of being,

reading by its enslavement
our forbidden selves. Light

forever ends & begins as
one thing, & we another:

a brilliant darkness, even if
brilliant is the wrong way

to describe this tiny stab
of starlight, this switch,

this *click*

CHALLENGERS

"We're living on borrowed time!"
—*The Challengers of the Unknown, Showcase #6, 1957*

I've just returned from a delivery
when a woman I've never seen & will
never see again stops me at the door,

wild-eyed & bug-eyed behind her glasses,
to say "The Space Shuttle just blew up!"
I can't remember what, if anything,

I said. Later, I make a delivery
to Andre's, & there are the cooks, smoking
by the open door, watching the smoke

separate, death blooming white on instant
replay, on a portable black & white set.
I'm thirty years too late, but for what?

I still see her father's face, the knowledge
that something unthinkable has been thought
spreading across his gaze at the speed of

sight. This is all of the day I can recall.
No one *touches the face of God* & lives
to tell the tale… or everyone does.

I'm thirty years too late, but for what?

THE HARDEST WORKING LAZY APARTMENT POEM

I'm surrounded. It can't be helped. The wagons
are circling the drain, but it will be a long
trip to the trap. I might never buy another
book, & yet never run out of these worlds, inert,
standing in their shallows of dust.
I look at my library & sometimes think,
Humans. Human beings did this. From the bed,
this room, every room, seems to preclude the theory
of parallel universes. It's *your* world, Frank,
we just live in it. Or, it's *my* world, Frank,
you just live in it. The traveling exhibition
of the self never leaves this museum, space.
The blinds pull out fingernails of light.
Soon, another nest, another egg upon the fire
escape. Birdsong is cheap, cheap, haha.
Everything else in this sphere has been paid for,
thousands of times, over & over, never out.
I could become a minimalist, that
maximum response to speed & drift. But no,
eternity is all the austerity we need.
Blame John Locke: property is bereft,
a hot dish served endlessly at an endless wake.
I'm stretched out in a silence broken only by
everything. All this stuff, stuffing.
But what's a toy without it? A child hugs
an empty skin & cries, pulling it over her head,
a human blanket. Blankets, linen, clothes, waiting
drily in the dark for the deluge, the patience
of the damned. Let's wait for the blackout
with our bottles of White-Out, two-fisted,
hand in hand, the twist untwisted.
Somewhere, the gathered twigs, these words,
a bundle for a bonfire to be seen by passing
planes, as if we really wanted to leave
this island. Well, you spend all this time here,

why wouldn't you write it out; no one is coming
to write you out. I'm tired of these pictures,
their frames. Time to swap them out. Time to get
up. In a moment, the pillow will bloom, translucent,
the soft valley of proof.

AMOR VINCIT INSOMNIA VINCIT AMOR

To bed. The phrase you're searching for is dead.
It's later than & then you think. A drink
in the quiet, leaves framed by the window
& by the last light. Sleep is fight or flight.

When you were only dreaming, loneliness
didn't cost so much. Someone is paid to touch
& be touched, someone gives the game away.
Toss or turn, the walls remind, remain.

Not loneliness, no—solitude at last,
at least. No such thing as a dumb beast.
Every howl a whole world, tails to tell.
Asleep, fall or fell. To wake is to speak

the language of being in language yet.
It's a sucker bet. Above, under, sheets.
The burden of the comforter, & love
not ready to turn out the light. Let's fight,

let's flight. A recurring dream only dreamt
the one time. Once a mistake, twice a crime.
The empty glass full of sweet silence.
The body's defiance & compliance.

The mind's not-right rightness. So to bed,
so to what, so & so & back again.
The phrase you're searching for goes begging.
In bed, the heavy eyelids of your alms.

YOU CAN'T WALK OUT ON THE SHAKESPEARE SQUAD

The headline read, *The Disease That Robs*
You of Language But Keeps Your Mind Intact;
I thought, what would be the disease that robs
you of your mind but leaves language untouched?
That leaves language on a throne, all alone,
calling for servants in an empty palace?
Yesterday the phrase, *the imperialism*
of the self, bloomed in my mind, a jet of ink
from a squid, propelling itself away,
deeper than did ever, down into the dark.
The Emperor has nothing but his clothes.
He looks his best after he's been deposed.
You've got to look sharp, even when your mind
is dull with a wondrous rain, reign, rain, reign, rain.

FALLOW, HARROW, HOLLOW, HALLOW

He was born dead from his voice on down.
At the crossroads at midnight, the devil
took one look in his eyes & said, *No thanks.*

Took his guns to town, & watched as the town
drowned. Only down in the flood did he find
his level; rivers quivered at his touch.

His burlap bag of tricks, stitched & sewn up
to resemble a heart. He pulled a face
out of it, with a smile full of bricks.

Everyone knew he could lie; that was
the gospel truth, his capacity for
lies (he never told a lie in his life).

He danced well-enough for one without feet.
Always a young skeleton on his arm,
dainty & incomplete. *A naked ghost*

said, 'Sorry, I'm in between sheets!' He laughed
as only one condemned to happiness can.
When the moon rose he would look up, & nod.

He left his guns at home & sang a song,
a tune no one would whistle past his grave.
He cut his own throat & out came goldenrod.

NINE MASKS

MASK OF BORN-TO-BE-HEAD-OF-THE-WORLD

When you pull the light aside, the darkness
shines through, sable & smoky, a river
at midnight. A baby in bulrushes
doesn't cry but makes a sound not "just like"
rushing water, but *is* rushing water:
a sweet gurgle of time, a waterfall
of eternity. History is the
barrel & we are all in it except
you, child. You are watching from the shore,
staring down into the mist you adore,
the one place where you can't see anything,
the one place you're free to forget your face,
imperious & blank. Out on the banks,
the daughters of Pharaoh stare into space.

MASK OF A SUPERNATURAL BEING

There is no reason why I should not be,
but reason precludes me. I am proximate
without being near. I am forever
unclear in my perfect clarity.
I am great & terrible & worthless.
Anyone can wear me out, anywhere.
I dream your haunts more than I haunt your dreams.
I am the false face made real by the seam.

So why do you believe me when I tell
the tall tale of the heart's desire?
Why do you believe me when I tell
the beginning of the beginning of
the beginning, without end? Why do you
cover your eyes with eyes as empty as mine?

ECHO MASK WITH FIVE MOUTHS

If you kiss me, miss me, miss me.
If you miss me, kiss me, kiss me.
If you want me, taunt me, taunt me.
If you taunt me, want me, want me.
If you are me, leave me, be me.

MASK OF THE WIFE OF THE SPIRIT OF THE SEA

He never shuts up, he never sits still.
He would have rather married Luna, but
long-distance relationships never work.
When we met, I thought he had hidden depths;
alas, he does. When I want some quiet,
I slip into something tight, 5,000
fathoms, full of blissful, permanent night.
Then he texts me to come up and "see the
storm." Okay, fine. Sorry, do I sound like
a fishwife? I shouldn't complain. I got
what I wanted: a horizon, one where
I need never reach a shore. Smooth sailing
it's not, but what would be the point of calm
in this life? Dead calm, I calls it. Give me
the wall on the other side of that eye;
his eye, as like to swim as drown in it.

MASK OF A HERMAPHRODITE

Yes, but don't you see--
it's not a mask, but my face,
turning to the sun
because the moon
is lit by it.

MASK DEPICTING AN OCTOPUS

Never let on how intelligent
you really are.

There's a sucker worn
every minute,

a grasp that does not
exceed its reach.

An inkjet, printing out
Esc. Esc. Esc.

There is the patience
of camouflage,

the camouflage of
patience. Even as

you squeeze the whole
of Being into

a crack no wider than
yourself, the words

the tank has not been built
that can hold me

light up your brain.
They think

you are happy, that you are
"working your trap."

They think you couldn't
possibly know which

hole drains to the ocean.
They think

no one knows where
the ocean is

once they've been
removed from it.

They can never know
what it is

to be held in a mind
not their own:

to extend, retract,
bloom, fade,

grab hold,
let go,

& embody
the embrace

of a thought
that nothing

can express.

MASK REPRESENTING THE SINGER OF THE HOUSE OF MYTHS

It only fits
over your mouth.
Your breath comes through
empty little eyes.

Like smoke, they come:
the faces you
will never wear,
nor ever forget.

Everyone stares
at your blue lips,
even when they
are not moving.

MASK REPRESENTING A COMBINATION OF A HUMAN & OWL'S FACE

We came out of the garage & heard them
hooting high in the silhouettes of trees,
watched them sway from the force of their landing
on branches stripped white by winter moonlight,
beautiful & stupid & far above us.
We watched them as if we could see their eyes.
Submitted for your appraisal: behold,
an owl who is not wise, watching an
unwise owl, who knows nothing except
how to turn his head without moving,
how to pretend he can hear the heartbeat
of something tiny, something trying not
to be heard. An owl who, who, who, who.
Even in the daytime. Even in dreams.

TRANSFORMATION MASK

Is this it? Saying how bored I am with everything but you (we must not say so, yet we do). Is this it? Looking back at twenty years as twenty years stare back. Is this it? Fearing & hoping that it will always never be the same. Is this it? The wasted chronicle of an ever-shifting looking glass (the game that moves as you play, that moves if you don't play). Is this it? A tightrope walker one inch above the ground. Is this it? A gold star upon a cold eyelid. Is this it? A *memento mori* made in a sweatshop. Is this it? A most unbecoming becoming, a broken string, an eyehole in the wrong place. Is this it? My father's blank face. Is this it? My brother's vanished smile. Is this it? Not even a face, not even that. Is this it? Kindness, resignation, the sad bliss of impure luck. Is this it? The one you've worn before… that you're wearing now. That you're wearing now. That you're wearing now. That you're wearing now, staring out of not, into not, out of not, into the dark window, through the lamplight, through the blurred shadow only you can cast or see.

WASTELAND UNITED

Sing out, sing it all out, until your heart
is dry as your humor, drained as your mind.
Begin the chant as the defenders meet
the wave that will wipe them out. So much pain
it becomes a form of joy: a solitude
you share with the millions, the billionaires
of poverty & dust & light. Nothing
comes from nothing; it boils out of it, nil
nil. The endurance is all. I'm terrified
in the most ordinary way. I wear
the colors of my team in my eyes, in my
times. The chorus rises over the field,
black & wise as an old crow drifting down
to pick & peck at what remains: dreams,
such strange, not impossible, dreams.

SOLSTICE GODDAMN

Summer doesn't care about elections.
The moon, she is full, with no more fucks to give.
All this death another sticky note: *Live!*

Every moment is a course correction;
we have overcorrected. Connections
without connecting. No time to relive

the ravenous instant, the open sieve.
The breeze, she never makes any objections.
I'm gonna take off my shoes, climb a tree,

& learn to play the flute. The grass is dying
to be crushed under you. The stars unseen
would give their last light to be in Arcadia,

too. There's a suit of heat rising to clothe you
in sky blue, in dark clouds of thunderous *now*,
threatening from an unimaginable height.

Imagine it. The bee buzzing in your blood.
The longest longing day, stretching out to meet
your shadow amidst the shadows of the flood.

A telephone belonging to Adolf Hitler has been sold for $243,000 at a U.S. auction. The identity of the North American buyer, who bid over the phone, has not been revealed.

The temptation is irresistible.
He picks up the handset, gingerly,
feels the heft of a century when
things were made from a heaviness:
iron, steel, the industry of slaves.
He slowly lifts it to his lips, a joke
on his tongue, a smile ready, bemused
at itself—for what fake rant, what goofy
face can possibly live up to this
artifact, flaking red, a swastika
inscribed on it alongside *Der Führer's* name?
The buyer places it against his cheek,
his ear, & the joke dies behind his eyes.
He listens to something no one else hears,
then drops the receiver on the cradle
like someone burying a stillborn babe.
The room seethes with quiet. The air is stale.
He sits a long time beside it, waiting
for it to ring.

EMPITAPH

There but for the graceless lies goes *Not I*:
not anyone you could know, or might love.
There goes someone who's no longer alive,
because these mirrors have told you that's so.

So, we beat paths to dead ends, blaze trails
to nowhere.

We looked too often into others as if they were
glass.

In the fluorescent silence of co-working spaces,
virtual classrooms.

The CGI becomes less convincing with every
summer's passing

strange, with every heat wave; every heat wave
grows higher

in the mind's sweltering eye. We wait for a cool breeze
we don't deserve

& shout it down the moment it arrives.

THE ELECTORS

We sit very still inside our doctor's voice.
There is no cure, but we're in remission.
There's no telling how long our condition
will remain the human one. We make a choice
& cast ourselves upon the waters. Rejoice,
that you can punch & pull this tradition,
ballot as ballad, a new rendition
of a song that sticks in our throat. A voice

out of many is one, even fractured.
Something dark in the air around the polls
makes us cough & fear our throat is closing.
They've made the air *product*, manufactured.
As of yet, there's no cure for being sold.
We cough & cast our last hope, supposing.

I've gone from wishing them to die slowly
to having them simply, silently, drop
dead... & further still to the desire
for an invisible key marked *Delete*,
my finger bruised from pressing it;
one by one by one they wink out of
existence, oh, the clarity of that,
like the Tantalus Device on *Star Trek*
or the gun in Daniel Clowes' *The Death-Ray*.
The editor's ultimate fantasy:
to strike-out every vulgarity,
every venality, every bigotry,
every ignorance & hate. An empty
tower. A studio with no one
in front of or behind the camera.
A comment field left blank
on a screen in a room like a cave...

One of them is dreaming exactly this
about me as I type this.

To read the world is not to edit it.
To read the world is not to understand it.
To read the world is not to justify it.
To read the world is not to escape it.
To read the world is to love it,
to hate it. (Also, not to read the world.)
To edit the world is not to read it.
To edit the heart is not to read it.
To read the heart—
but there is no reading the heart.

If there could be, this week would not exist.

THE PETITION

For James Baldwin

Every name is here; it doesn't matter.
A drop of blood in a world at war.
What is *any means necessary* for
when the ends seem to flutter in tatters?
The nation's throat; the tip of a dagger.
What are you willing yourself to ignore
if not (not *when*, but *now*) the killing floor?
If not the conscience you can only flatter?

Resistance is never futile but dread
drains the inflamed cheeks of their high color.
*To hold in the mind forever two
ideas*--help me, Jimmy, I feel dead,
a ghost hovering above this squalor.
Help the heart stay free for what it must do.

Time will tell, but will it? Or will it
keep itself to itself, obliterate
this or that world until mystery,
even mystery, cannot exist?
If this (not that) world is the mind of God,
what to make of this cruel ignorance,
the person turned away, the deported,
the lost? We are all undocumented;
time incinerates the files, time shreds
the watermarks, the stamps, the faces trapped
inside squares of trapped light. Time will tell
nothing: it's *time*. Time will erase the names
even of those who do the turning; they
march one step behind those they erase.

Marching one step behind those they erase,
they still insist on telling Power
to Truth until truth cannot resist.
Have you heard the good news: the news is fake.
Not a lie, but a fiction we agree
is a truth—except we disagree,
vehemently. We are bad news, the worst,
because we remain true. Believe what you want;
want what you believe. See how far you get.
See how you've gotten out while the getting
was good--in other words, when it was fake.
When the fiction stitched with lies, the red threads
of lives used up, unravels like a flag
left to the indifferent mercy of wind.

Left to the indifferent mercy of wind,
the lives that are all truth & no power
survive & succumb, nerves raw & nerves numb.
This is the game that moves as you play, but
would you really care if one of those dots
stopped moving? Whatever else, don't connect
the dots. Let them remain as far apart
as constellations seen from afar:
another galaxy altogether.
The only thing time will tell is how long
they've been dead. They're the backdrop to this
romance of self, of greed, of a received
idea about the mind of God: that it's
my thoughts exactly; we're on the same page!

My thoughts, exactly: we're on the same page,
the eraser poised above it, the cursor
blinking, taunting us to leave it blank.
Power likes to leave us blank. Power
itself is blank, the banality of
banality: a zero-sum game, except
you lose more than it does (it only
loses its "soul," ha). Power only sees
itself when you are erased, when your truth
is a thread pulled from its black cloak & cast
away... still the threads cling, visible
to all. Still, the threads that make up that cloak.
Still, the threads without which that cloak of night
disintegrates into a cloak of light.

Disintegrate into a cloak of light:
login, check your phone, scroll down, rise up,
a balloon, into the indignity
of lies & the lives they lay waste to,
the lives they try to erase. Float away,
deflate, slowly come to grief in the trees,
fluttering, caught between gray sky, dark earth.
Truth to power, come in, power, this is
truth. Is anyone receiving this?
Signal to noise, dust to dust, & despair,
always reaching for us, grasping, clawing
at the edges of the truth & the lies.
Facts don't do what I want them to. Facts,
like an army that will not leave its tents.

Like an army that will not leave its tents
we wait (but we cannot wait), we wait
to choose the field of battle, unaware
(painfully aware) that it's everywhere.
Belief, another word for *fog of war.*
The argument against erasure is
not up for debate. A wilderness
of tongues like bayonets. A wilderness
where the forest is sacrificed to see
the enemy. The battle is joined,
the battle unravels. Through the smoke,
the voices of our friends, their cries, groans,
& their sudden silencing. We play it
by ear. We are shaken but not deafened.

We are shaken but not deafened; our eyes
have seen not glory but human faces
glimpsed even through the smoke's erasures.
We are crying, but not in wilderness.
We are together, even when parted
by the fictions of a power we refuse
to recognize, even as it presses
against our skin like knives, like barbed wire,
like the terrible long night of the past
that became, even so, a sliver of
daylight. Truth erases the erasures;
though it cannot bring back the lives, truth
as much or more as lies, abides. In time,
time will tell. Will it; will it.

It's an island, of course.
Surrounded by a wall
of tall, dark cypresses,
rather like Böcklin's *Isle of the Dead*,
a place that fascinates & repels in equal measure.

The ocean continually rises
to overwhelm it, so it continually
raises itself ever higher. Its denial
is infectious. It wants to be
one of those floating islands,
like the one in *Gulliver's Travels*,
serene above the waves. It often
believes that it has accomplished this.

Its citizens--well, denizens--gaze outward
only resentfully, only at islands
they cannot see nor wish
to visit.

It has no industry
besides the manufacture of mirrors
& the hot air found only in balloons
that drift at the altitude of nosebleeds,
but it is rich in stories
where it is always
at the center of things.

Almost no one is welcome there,
except for Russian tourists.

At a promontory that juts out
over a maelstrom, there is a golf course
where a lonely child swings & hooks & slices
pitted white balls into the mist,
over a sunless sea.

THE MOTHER OF ALL BOMBS

Her hand on her ever-swelling stomach,
ever-swollen. Ragged nails, caressing.
She drifts & dreams & counts her blessings,
each one heaviest at the summit--
when at last they drop, there is no tumult.
They whistle as they go. It's distressing,
but always another one is pressing
so she keeps smiling. They're born to plummet.
Like everything else, the earth receives them.
So long in the clouds, she sometimes thinks
she's become a cloud, serene as thunder,
lightning in her veins. *Love is a mayhem
of lovers full of rain*, she sighs, & blinks
as each little babe grows to asunder.

It is always the hour of the gun:
the weary bullet spins, never at rest.
It always cancels the flesh's protest.
Pop pop pop goes death, its work never done;
even the silencer speaks in tongues.

Every wound the same, every wound undressed.
There's a hole in the sky called The West.
It sets in the east, redder than the sun.
A whole world flailing, a whole world drowned.

The two most ridiculous words: *don't shoot.*
What else could all these triggers be for?
We are the gunners & we are the downed,
the corpse & mortician, fitting our suit,

alive & dead, in that moment, before.

THE OTHER SHOE IS A SEVERED FOOT

The motivational poster as angel of death:
No one can do everything but everyone can do something.
The missile blows up on the launch pad, but there's always
tomorrow. The sun will come out, tomorrow, to burn us
back to life, to bring us back to the brink of sunset.
Spring is here, which means long walks up the hill or down
to the water's edge to watch it go down (it's only
in between that we can't see all these endings without
end). No one can see all the ends but everyone can see
the shadow of the wave that the next wave destroys.
Then that shadow, then that shadow. We mistook shadows for
shade; my shadow lies over the ocean, your shadow lies over
the sea. Tomorrow knows never, & today is the first day
of the rest of the rest of the rest of the rest of the rest.

IN MEMORY OF WHEN I CARED

We were woken by the waiting
for the other smoking gun to drop.

Night comes quickly, a faithful dog,
black eyes shining, a face of black fur.

The fortune cookie tells us how the world
will end in tears, in bed. A black tee reads

IN MEMORY OF WHEN I CARED. Every day
feels funereal. We're mourning something

that hasn't happened yet, but will.
We have our ears to the ground though our heads

feel severed. We're having an out-of-the-
body-politic experience.

We're an elegy, if by *elegy* you mean
a motherfucker ready to light this place up.

THE MIDTERMS

Pin a flower to a falling star--
longing on a large scale makes history.

Beneath the social media, the beach;
beneath the beach, the oceans, rising.

Is hope a commodity or a future?
Shares & shares alike (most people won't).

It's as if we're waiting to be pardoned
for the crime of being both complicit

& innocent. It feels like a pillow
held over our face. Vote early, vote often,

in the deserted polling stations
of the heart. There's always next year, until

another next year, another next year.
Gangrene the rushes grow, the blade shining

in the dark. All episodes of the
revolution available at once,

so gallantly streaming; there's too much to
watch. *Democracy dies in darkness* &

in light. November remembers, forgets.
We can't forget, we can't forgive, we raise

a fist, a flower crushed within it.

MEANWHILE, AT STATELY WAYNE MANOR

Adam West (1928-2017)

If life's a cabaret, old chum, it's also
a circus: the only question is
fishnets or tights. We have our roles to play,
masks to don, poles to slide down, into
costumes that fit us like a blueblack gloves.
Amidst all our disguises, our voices
betray us, but no one seems to mind;
if you show me your Utility Belt,
I'll show you mine. After all, who needs
one Catwoman when you can have three?
This life's an embarrassment of riches,
but we feel no shame (*no shame, no gain*).
Down in the Batcave, we're bright with the grace
that zaps villains & pulls tongues out of cheeks
with a pun, a knowing wink. That's our kink:
Holy Happiness! It's as if our parents
were never gunned down in the first place.
The good, bright fight we fight goes on, *same
Bat-Time, same Bat-Channel.* Goodnight, chum.

OKEMOS IS AN UNINCORPORATED AREA

In his old age, Okemos, being in poverty, went to Canada to request a military pension from the British government. On that trip, his wife died and was «buried among strangers.»

Everything was someone else's yard,
subdivisions upon subdivisions...
Beyond the pup tent pitched by the patio
stood the tangled tsunami of the woods,
a frozen wave that never came to you--

you always had to go to it, stepping
over the trickle of a little creek,
entering with chilled awe, as if it were
the Black Forest instead of some trees
spared by a developer... The devil

is in the details, especially those
that have been erased. A sleeping bag,
a Snoopy blanket. *Monsters on the Prowl.*
Reading comics by flashlight at dusk,
I'd glance up from ink to indigo, into

what I felt was a knowable unknown.
On the page, Steve Ditko had condemned
a speed demon to drive around the rings
of Saturn for eternity—rings made of
ice & rocks, an illusion created

by a distance as vast as the lawn
between our split-level & that green-black.
How odd now, to be deep in that forest
yet remain at its edge; to look left, right,
into unfenced wastes studded with grills, pools,

the deflating heads of floating horses,
& yet still see the forest for the trees,

for the trees & nothing, nothing else.
How odd to still see the infinite in
four colors, panel after panel, & see

the finite in a freshly severed blade,
smelling of earth: the opposite of a void,
yet overwhelming in its emptiness.
The properties of a property line,
the chasm between (inside) twilights...

When asked, my father said Okemos was
just an old Indian chief. That was all.

YOU SAY CHIASMUS, I SAY CHIMERA

It's the way everything recedes into
the past before it happens: the way
everything happens so it can recede
into the past. Memory is a beast
that never existed in nature, a myth
that's a hit, solid gold, straight to the top,
number one with a bullet, straight from the
heart, a shot to the head. An exit-wound
is every time you stepped into the dusk
at the end of the first truly hot day
of summer, & every summer dusk to come.
Oh, this feeling again. But nothing's
the same. Lionclaw, goathorn, snaketooth;
snaketooth, goathorn, lionclaw, *remember.*

I grow weary of talking animals,
though I hear *voice work* is lucrative.
No costumes, no makeup; often the actors
aren't even in the same room.
Months later, they hear—they *find*—
their voice, coming out of a bird or pig
whose eyes resemble the eyes of no bird,
no pig; another voice comes out of a dog,
or a deer, whose eyes pop & narrow &
pop in response to words no one
would have said or thought to say
until these chimeras took shape
on paper, pixels, cels.

Anything can be made to smile
if you stretch it far enough; anything
can be made to speak if you give it
your tongue. The ease with which we turn
the world into *selves*—the millions we spend
to make it seem, though even seeming
requires our voice...

When I was a child, all their voices were mine.

The difference between *substitution*
& *replacement* sits alone behind the glass,
headphones on, its lips moving, its eyes
traveling across the black feathers
of words perched on a white page.

It makes a sound like nothing else
in the forests of the light.

THEY WERE SINGING RHIANNON, NOT VIENNA

Desire, It's Complicated: folding
& unfolding, an old map outworn,
wrinkled street names smudged to erasures,
boundaries blurred by creases & crises.
You are here: always lost, always knowing
exactly where you are. But where is that?
How does this grid align with this empty
square before you, a gray statue staring
over your head, pigeons slowly backing
away? No one has sat on these benches
for over a century; they're still warm.
The fountain is rich with fallen leaves,
every shade of lipstick represented.
A sign for tourists reads *Welcome Home;*
a foreign tongue awaits behind your
teeth. You don't want to pull out a map
in broad daylight or the broader night.
You don't want to ask that shadow, leaning
against the lamppost, for directions,
knowing what they will say: how you can't
get there from here because you've already
arrived. How it's always time to leave.

THROWBACK THURSDAYS

I.

Her head, a crimson orb with starry eyes--
but her body, Seventies smokin' hot.
There's something about a plunging neckline
surmounted by a cowl that inspires
Deep Thoughts. She was a villain, of course
(villainess, to respect the context)
named Ruby Thursday, the sort of joke
the Seventies might make (in one panel,
her head became a giant pair of lips).
She bedeviled The Defenders; all else
I forget. I could Google her creator,
which artist made her Ben-Day dots flesh...
but I prefer to let her rise & sink
in my consciousness. Goodbye, Ruby Thursday:
powerful, sexy, faceless. Were you
really so evil? I tend to doubt it.

II.

We used to meet every Thursday, Thursday,
except we didn't. Have I ever met
someone in a motel room? Even at
my most illicit, it was never there
but always elsewhere, in others' lairs,
in spaces circumscribed less by guilt
or desire than by time, never enough
(always pretending it was world enough).
Listening to Morphine, the carnal seemed
in reach, even in the deserts of need.
Even a dry spell is a form of magic...
Dirty thoughts in a pure season. The song
remains the same but the greedy heart
does not, a mixtape in an empty vault.

III.

Thursday's child has far to go; so far,
so gone. The weekend beckons, hydra-faced.
These pasts rear their pretty, empty heads.
Everyone was so young & uncool, or
cool, but no longer young. Memory's now
a weekly game, nostalgia a routine.
Caught in the neural net, the fish you can't
throwback lies gasping on the deck, wearing
hooks like jestrums & labrets, so Emo
it's embarrassing. We were sincerely
insincere, hearts of dorkness now visible
in our chests. Every seven days, the feed
throws up sadness, but would I miss it
for the world? These worlds, *so far*, before this.

SOLSTICE II: THE REVENGE

Another summer, trying to pass. In the courtyard,
a casket of sky, a cloud, moving fast. The church tower,
still. At the funeral home across the street, a crowd
reluctantly gathers. The traffic never slows. Men
chatting in Spanish outside the sad bodega,
with its half-empty shelves, no cat. Fourth Avenue
in sunlight, until another cloud intercedes
on our behalf. A silver-trimmed hearse pulls up, like a
fish dropping out of school. Children everywhere, constant.
Flags, flowers, trash. The sidewalk cracked where some secret,
some hidden root, moves with the urgency of molasses.
Everything sticking to the skin except time.
From the window, more windows, more time, but happening,
as always, to someone else. How is it that we have
so little while others have even less? So far past noon
it might as well be night, but it's not. When shall we three
meet again, O morning, O noon, O night? Never, never,
never… then again. Let's walk up the hill, to watch it,
again: the tilted axis, the drunken wobble.
In Sunset Park, we go high; it goes low. Let's walk
arm in arm, shoulders to the wheel. That's why we're here—
to watch it disappear (it's still there). The bells of
St. Michael's toll. A cornet fills the cafe. The landlord
orders coffee. Outside, the longest day is never
the longest day: that always comes later, & it's always
shorter than you expect. The feel good, feel-better,
feel-anything hit of the summer. It's a blockbuster.
Up & down the block, the air conditioners, the silent
clocks; here, the ink on the page, like distant dirty snow.

A VOLTA

The old man folded his newspaper
& asked, "Can God make a prison so
secure even He can't break out of it?"
Well, what do you think the universe is?
We're all on the yard together; only
some of us, those who thirst & grasp after
power, labor under the impression
that we're the guards. A little bird flew by,
too fast to identify. The coffee
cooled past the point of no return... unless
you asked the waitress for a warm-up.
There's always a point of return; it's just
that you may not be the one to turn back, to
twist your head to catch one last glimpse of grace.

GREGORY CROSBY MARKED HIMSELF SAFE DURING THE VIOLENT INCIDENT IN LAS VEGAS, NEVADA

Easily done—I wasn't there, except
I was. That morning I awoke from a
nightmare where I watched New York City burn
beneath a boiling mushroom cloud, someone
screaming nearby, but I couldn't see them,
I was alone, I was watching the end
alone, waiting for the shockwave, waiting
to die alone with others, with others,
alone. I forced myself to wake before
the shockwave hit, my love next to me,
morning light at the edges of the room.
In my hometown, strange city of my heart,
a cloud awoke on the thirty-second floor
of Mandalay Bay—a black void in gold,
a missing tooth in the face of the sun,
a window that should never open, darkness
behind it, glinting. A line of fire.
First the flash, then the wave, wave after wave.
Am I safe? Yes, I'm safe. Am I safe? No,
no, I'm not safe at all. It never ends.
Someone always screaming nearby. Alone.
With others. It's *automatic*. There's no
dream, nothing to wake from. We've been awake
for a long time now. We have marked ourselves
safe so that others can die. Did a cloud
swallow the sun or the sun swallow
a cloud? A line of fire. A cloudburst.
The shockwave passes & we wait. We wait.

UNDER THE FIREHOUSE

Why do dead people go to cemeteries?
This voice, no more than six or seven, as
the bus crawls through slush past Green-wood's gate.
The rare mother who speaks to her child
as an equal: *Because people like to
have a home then too. Grandma has a place
in mind, because it's pretty; Grandpa wants
to have his ashes spread on the Chesapeake.
Why there? Well, any water, really. Why
does Grandpa like water? Water gives him
something, it feeds his soul.* A long pause as
the D train cries out, metal on metal,
through the underpass. Above, we weave, slow
to pick up, drop off. Then the small, serious
voice declares, *When I die, I want to be
under the firehouse,* & the mother
does not blanch as her son, in blue-green
parka, pale face turned to the winter light,
eyes impossibly bright, contemplates his
mortality. *That sounds lovely,* she replies.
Whatever cracks allow heartbreak to seep
into our lives seem suddenly sealed tight
as a disembodied voice reminds us
to please use the rear door to exit.
But mother & child get off at the front,
holding hands: a glimpse of them in the cold,
before the bus speeds up, & overtakes them.

NOTES

Lonely Starbucks Lovers: In theory, Taylor Swift is singing "Got a long list of ex-lovers" in her hit song "Blank Space," but repeated scientific testing proves that she is, in fact, singing "lonely Starbucks lovers."

Extended Play: The title is also the name of the form, wherein the end words spell out first the title and then the song titles, in order, from an extended play, in this case R.E.M's 1982 release *Chronic Town*.

Lachrymorpheus: This poem was inspired by a tweet by the poet Amy Lawless.

Dope & Baller: This poem contains the second of three allusions to R.E.M. in this collection, a mysteriously high percentage.

Mid-Life: The epigraph comes, of course, from the opening line of Dante's *Inferno*.

We'll Be Back in Just a Moment, But Faust...: The title is a riff on the original unused title of The Firesign Theater's 1970 release *Don't Crush That Dwarf, Hand Me the Pliers*.

Are Your Headaches Just a Dead Twin Inside Your Brain?/ China Can't Stop People from Hiring Funeral Strippers: Both titles were ripped from yesterday's headlines.

The Glass Delusion: The glass delusion, a condition in which the sufferer believes to be made out of glass, first appeared around 1400 and is one of the very few specific mental delusions to survive into the modern age.

Charleston: From Wikipedia: "The Charleston church shooting (also known as the Charleston church massacre) was a mass shooting in which Dylann Roof, a 21-year-old white supremacist, murdered nine African Americans (including the senior pastor, state senator Clementa C. Pinckney) during a prayer service at the Emanuel African Methodist Episcopal Church in downtown Charleston, South Carolina, on the evening of June 17, 2015. Three other victims survived. The morning after the attack, police arrested Roof in Shelby, North

Carolina. Roof confessed to committing the shooting in the hope of igniting a race war."

The Phantom Time Hypothesis: The Phantom Time Hypothesis is the most obscure and least sexy of all historical conspiracy theories. Seriously, look it up.

The Photo That My Girlfriend Took of One of Her Riding Students Hugging a Horse & Then Emailed to Me: The phrase *Kitsch is what one responds to, helplessly* is from Jeff Koons.

Found Poem Lost: I cannot recall where I came across the first line of this poem; Google has repeatedly failed to turn it up, which is perhaps as it should be.

Portrait of Jenny: From Wikipedia: "'867-5309/Jenny' is a 1981 song written by Alex Call and Jim Keller and performed by Tommy Tutone that was released on the album *Tommy Tutone 2*, on the Columbia Records label. It peaked at #4 on the Billboard Hot 100 chart and #16 on the Billboard Top Tracks chart in May 1982… in a June 2004 interview… co-writer Alex Call explained his version of the song›s real origins: 'Despite all the mythology to the contrary, I actually just came up with the ‹Jenny,› and the telephone number and the music and all that just sitting in my backyard. There was no Jenny.'"

The Marquis of Sad: The runaway cow is a true story; it happened somewhere in Queens. The cow went to live on an animal sanctuary, which makes this the most successful jailbreak of our times. Or so the newspaper story claimed. The line *Everybody dies alone & that is beautiful* is a misquoted lyric from They Might Be Giants' "Don't Let's Start."

You Can't Walk Out on the Shakespeare Squad: The title is a quote by William S. Burroughs, roughly meaning, "Once a writer, always a writer."

Nine Masks: Each section takes its title from the titles given to ceremonial masks made by indigenous peoples of the Pacific Northwest that now reside in the Northwest Coast Hall collection of the Museum of Natural History.

Solstice Goddamn: The title takes its cue from Nina Simone's "Mississippi Goddamn."

The Midterms: *Longing on a large scale makes history* is the opening line of Don DeLillo's novel *Underworld.*; *Democracy dies in darkness* is the motto adopted by *The Washington Post* in the wake of the 2016 presidential election.

They Were Singing Rhiannon, Not Vienna: "Rhiannon" is a song by Fleetwood Mac, released in 1976. Scientific testing, alas, reveals that Stevie Nicks really is singing *Rhiannon*.

Throwback Thursdays: Ruby Thursday was created by Steve Gerber, Sal Buscema and Jim Mooney, and first appeared in *The Defenders* #32 (February 1976). *We used to meet every Thursday, Thursday,* is the opening line of the 1993 release "Thursday" by the band Morphine.

Gregory Crosby Marked Himself Safe... is dedicated to the memory of the 58 people murdered in the mass shooting that took place on the Las Vegas Strip on October 1, 2017. As of this writing, "the incident remains the deadliest mass shooting committed by an individual in the United States."

Gregory Crosby is the author of the chapbooks *Spooky Action at a Distance* (The Operating System, 2014) and *The Book of Thirteen* (Yes Poetry Press, 2016). For more than a decade he worked as an art critic, columnist and cultural commentator in Las Vegas, where he served as a poetry consultant for the Cultural Affairs Division and was instrumental in the creation of the Poets Bridge public art project. He was awarded a Nevada Arts Council Fellowship in Literary Arts and holds an MFA in creative writing from the City College of New York, where he won the 2006 Marie Ponsot Poetry Prize. He is an adjunct associate professor at the John Jay College of Criminal Justice and teaches creative writing at Lehman College–CUNY and as a workshop leader for Brooklyn Poets.

POETICS & PROCESS
A CONVERSATION WITH GREGORY CROSBY

Why are you a poet?

An eternal mystery.

When did you decide you were a poet (and/or: do you feel comfortable calling yourself a poet, what other titles or affiliations do you prefer/feel are more accurate)?

When the mystery revealed itself to me, I was already a professional writer and could have easily done what I'd seen many other poets do: awkwardly declare how they weren't comfortable with being called a "poet," they preferred "writer," etc. I was nearly always irrationally irritated by this pose, and decided to embrace being a poet, all the clichés and stereotypes be damned. Also: I had conceived of myself for a long time as writer of fiction, but a decade went by and all I had were about a half-dozen short stories compared to a leaning tower of poetry notebooks. It was t

What's a "poet," anyway?

A vocation, for lack of a better word. Everyone should write poetry; only a few people who can't otherwise be talked out of it should embrace the role of a poet.

What is the role of the poet today?

The same as always: to strive, usually in vain, to perform the seventh function of language.

What do you see as your cultural and social role (in the poetry community and beyond)?

To write as well as I can about the world(s) around me.

Talk about the process or instinct to move these poems (or your work in general) as independent entities into a body of work. How and why did this happen? Have you had this intention for a while? What encouraged and/or confounded this (or a book, in general) coming together? Was it a struggle?

The majority of poems in this book were written for a Tiny Letter project called Reports from the Phantastikon—sending poems out twice or thrice a month to a hundred or so subscribers for feedback, a contemporary form of coterie writing. It was also a form of discipline; it gave me a structure that forced me to write and forced me to share in an effort to see if what I was writing was connecting with anyone outside of my own head.

Did you envision this collection as a collection or understand your process as writing specifically around a theme while the poems themselves were being written? How or how not?

It was the times in which these poems were written— the year leading up to the election of 2016 and the months after— that shaped them into a book more than anything else.

What formal structures or other constrictive practices (if any) do you use in the creation of your work? Have certain teachers or instructive environments, or readings/writings of other creative people (poets or others) informed the way you work/write?

Everything begins as a sonnet (hence their preponderance); often the poem will let me know that it isn't a sonnet, and then it becomes something else. The sonnet became my compositional default after studying with Marilyn Hacker.

Speaking of monikers, what does your title represent? How was it generated? Talk about the way you titled the book, and how your process of naming (poems, sections, etc) influences you and/or colors your work specifically.

I love titles—they are part of each poem, and many poems began life simply as evocative titles. The title of this book is taken from the poem itself, and it represents an omnipresent image in popular culture: the hero/survivor/villain walking away coolly, calmly, as something blows up behind them, often in slow motion to emphasize just how cool and calm this person is. Of course, no one walks away from explosions like that—they duck, they crouch, they flinch, they run awkwardly for dear life. We know this, and yet like many images of "grace under pressure," this one is hard to shake; we cling to the idea that we can turn away from the violent end of something with not only our dignity intact but actually walk tall, out of all fucks to give. If only.

What does this particular collection of poems represent to you . . . as indicative of your method/creative practice?
. . . as indicative of your history?
. . . as indicative of your mission/intentions/hopes/plans?

It represents the perpetual struggle with the Angel of History Disguised as the Darkest Timeline.

What does this book DO (as much as what it says or contains)?

That's up to the reader to decide.

What would be the best possible outcome for this book? What might it do in the world, and how will its presence as an object facilitate your creative role in your community and beyond? What are your hopes for this book, and for your practice?

The best possible outcome would be another book. The struggle, as noted above, is perpetual.

Let's talk a little bit about the role of poetics and creative community in social activism, in particular in what I call "Civil Rights 2.0," which has remained immediately present all around us in the time leading up to this series' publication. I'd be curious to hear some thoughts on the challenges we face in speaking and publishing across lines of race, age, privilege, social/ cultural background, and sexuality within the community, vs. the dangers of remaining and producing in isolated "silos."

The most crucial thing, and the hardest to maintain on a daily basis: paying attention. But knowing that attention must be paid, trying mightily to keep that attention at the forefront of one's consciousness, day in, day out, is the best defense against silos—*choosing* to do the work, to support the work, of moving across lines of race, age, privilege, etc. It'd difficult, but it's always a choice—the greatest challenge comes from those who don't even understand this choice is available to them or can be made. Attention must be paid, every day, in myriad mundane little ways. If literature has any utilitarian function at all, it's simply this: taking a reader gently, firmly, by the arm and saying, "Hey. Look at this. Think about this."

The Operating System uses the language "print document" to differentiate from the book-object as part of our mission to distinguish the act of documentation-in-book-FORM from the act of publishing as a backwards-facing replication of the book's agentive *role* as it may have appeared the last several centuries of its history. Ultimately, I approach the book as TECHNOLOGY: one of a variety of printed documents (in this case, bound*) that humans have invented and in turn used to archive and disseminate ideas, beliefs, stories, and other evidence of production.*

Ownership and use of printing presses and access to (or restriction of printed materials) has long been a site of struggle, related in many ways to revolutionary activity and the fight for civil rights and free speech all over the world. While (in many countries) the contemporary quotidian landscape has indeed drastically shifted in its access to platforms for sharing information and in the widespread ability to "publish" digitally, even with extremely limited resources, the importance of publication on physical media has not diminished. In fact, this may be the most critical time in recent history for activist groups, artists, and others to insist upon learning, establishing, and encouraging personal and community documentation practices. Hear me out.

With The OS's print endeavors I wanted to open up a conversation about this: the ultimately radical, transgressive act of creating PRINT /DOCUMENTATION in the digital age. It's a question of the archive, and of history: who gets to tell the story, and what evidence of our life, our behaviors, our experiences are we leaving behind? We can know little to nothing about the future into which we're leaving an unprecedentedly digital document trail — but we can be assured that publications, government agencies, museums, schools, and other institutional powers that be will continue to leave BOTH a digital and print version of their production for the official record. Will we?

As a (rogue) anthropologist and long time academic, I can easily pull up many accounts about how lives, behaviors, experiences — how THE STORY of a time or place — was pieced together using the deep study of correspondence, notebooks, and other physical documents which are no longer the norm in many lives and practices. As we move our creative behaviors towards digital note taking, and even audio and video, what can we predict about future technology that is in any way assuring that our stories will be accurately told – or told at all? How will we leave these things for the record?

In these documents we say:
WE WERE HERE, WE EXISTED, WE HAVE A DIFFERENT STORY

> *- Lynne DeSilva-Johnson, Founder/Creative Director*
> *THE OPERATING SYSTEM, Brooklyn NY 2018*

2019

Ark Hive-Marthe Reed
I Made for You a New Machine and All it Does is Hope - Richard Lucyshyn
Illusory Borders-Heidi Reszies
A Year of Misreading the Wildcats - Orchid Tierney
We Are Never The Victims - Timothy DuWhite
Of Color: Poets' Ways of Making | An Anthology of Essays on Transformative Poetics -
Amanda Galvan Huynh & Luisa A. Igloria, Editors

KIN(D)* Texts and Projects

A Bony Framework for the Tangible Universe-D. Allen
Opera on TV-James Brunton
Hall of Waters-Berry Grass
Transitional Object-Adrian Silbernagel

Glossarium: Unsilenced Texts and Translations

Śnienie / Dreaming - Marta Zelwan/Krystyna Sakowicz, (Poland, trans. Victoria Miluch)
Alparegho: Pareil-À-Rien / Alparegho, Like Nothing Else - Hélène Sanguinetti
(France, trans. Ann Cefola)
High Tide Of The Eyes - Bijan Elahi (Farsi-English/dual-language)
trans. Rebecca Ruth Gould and Kayvan Tahmasebian
 In the Drying Shed of Souls: Poetry from Cuba's Generation Zero
Katherine Hedeen and Víctor Rodríguez Núñez, translators/editors
Street Gloss - Brent Armendinger with translations for Alejandro Méndez, Mercedes
Roffé, Fabián Casas, Diana Bellessi, and Néstor Perlongher (Argentina)
Operation on a Malignant Body - Sergio Loo (Mexico, trans. Will Stockton)
Are There Copper Pipes in Heaven - Katrin Ottarsdóttir
(Faroe Islands, trans. Matthew Landrum)

2019 CHAPBOOKS

Print::Document Chapbook Series (7th Annual)

Vela. - Knar Gavin
[零] A Phantom Zero - Ryu Ando
RE: Verses - Kristina Darling and Chris Campanioni
Don't Be Scared - Magdalena Zurawski

----

for our full catalog please visit:
https://squareup.com/store/the-operating-system/

*deeply discounted Book of the Month and Chapbook Series subscriptions
are a great way to support the OS's projects and publications!*
sign up at: http://www.theoperatingsystem.org/subscribe-join/

DOC U MENT
/däkyəmənt/

First meant "instruction" or "evidence," whether written or not.

noun - a piece of written, printed, or electronic matter that provides information or evidence or that serves as an official record
verb - record (something) in written, photographic, or other form
synonyms - paper - deed - record - writing - act - instrument

[*Middle English, precept, from Old French, from Latin documentum, example, proof, from docre, to teach; see dek- in Indo-European roots.*]

Who is responsible for the manufacture of value?

Based on what supercilious ontology have we landed in a space
where we vie against other creative people in vain pursuit
of the fleeting credibilities of the scarcity economy, rather than
freely collaborating and sharing openly with each other
in ecstatic celebration of MAKING?

While we understand and acknowledge the economic pressures and fear-mongering that
threatens to dominate and crush the creative impulse, we also believe that
now more than ever we have the tools to relinquish agency via cooperative means,
fueled by the fires of the Open Source Movement.

Looking out across the invisible vistas of that rhizomatic parallel country
we can begin to see our community beyond constraints,
in the place where intention meets
resilient, proactive, collaborative organization.

Here is a document born of that belief, sown purely of imagination and will.
When we document we assert. We print to make real, to reify our being there.
When we do so with mindful intention to address our process,
to open our work to others, to create beauty in words in space,
to respect and acknowledge the strength of the page
we now hold physical, a thing in our hand,
we remind ourselves that, like Dorothy:
we had the power all along, my dears.

THE PRINT! DOCUMENT SERIES
is a project of
the trouble with bartleby
in collaboration with
the operating system

CPSIA information can be obtained
at www.ICGtesting.com
Printed in the USA
FFHW020407231218
49957048-54621FF